CACTUS

THE EARTH'S GARDEN

Jason Cooper

Rourke Enterprises, Inc.
Vero Beach, Florida 32964

PHOTO CREDITS

All Photographs © Lynn M. Stone

LIBRARY OF CONGRESS
Library of Congress Cataloging-in-Publication Data
Cooper, Jason, 1942-
  Cactus / by Jason Cooper.
  p. cm. — (The Earth's garden)
  Includes index.
  Summary: An introduction to cactuses, a plant family of some
2000 species which share the ability to store water.
  ISBN 0-86592-622-0
  1. Cactus—Juvenile literature.   [1. Cactus.]
I. Title.   II. Series: Cooper, Jason, 1942-   Earth's garden.
QK495.C11C66   1991
583'.47—dc20   91-7145
                             CIP
                             AC

TABLE OF CONTENTS

CACTUSES

"Ouch!" says the person who gets too close to a cactus plant. Most cactuses have spines. Spines are sharp. Some spines are straight, just like long needles. Others spines are hooked. Some are tiny, but all cactus spines can hurt.

Cactus plants look different than the other green plants with soft stems. A cactus may look like a barrel or a beaver tail. It may also look like deer antlers or a tree without leaves.

Barrel cactus with yellow fruit

CACTUS PARTS

Cactuses have the same main parts as other plants: flowers, stems, roots, and leaves.

The body of a cactus is its stem. Some stems grow in sections called **joints.** The branches of cholla (CHOY ah) cactus have many joints.

The spines of a cactus are its leaves. They help the plant in many ways. One way they help is to protect the soft, fleshy part of the plant from being eaten by animals.

Acuna cactus growing in Organ Pipe Cactus National Monument

NEW CACTUS PLANTS

Cactus flowers have several special parts. Each part has a job in helping cactuses to make new plants.

When a cactus flower dies, it is replaced by a fruit. Seeds grow in the fruit. New cactuses sprout from some of the seeds when they are buried.

A cactus plant can also grow from a cactus joint. If the joint of a cholla cactus fall to the ground, it may take root.

The bright flowers of Engelmann's hedgehog cactus

THE CACTUS FAMILY

The family of plants known as cactuses includes nearly 2,000 kinds, or **species.** Each species is somewhat different from all others. Still, all cactus plants share many features. One feature is the ability to soak up and store water. Water makes cactuses bulge into their strange shapes.

Several cactuses have names that help tell what the plant looks like. Some of them are hedgehog, fishhook, pincushion, organ pipe, and prickly pear.

Prickly pear cactus with flowers and fruit

Chain-fruit cholla cactus growing in southern Arizona

Prickly pear cactus fruits

CACTUS HOMES

Most cactuses live in **deserts.** Some kinds of cactuses live in grasslands, in jungles, along sandy coasts, and on mountainsides. A few kinds of cactuses live as far north as British Columbia, Canada, and Massachusetts.

The deserts, where most cactuses live, are too dry for most plants. Cactus plants, however, have special ways to survive. When rain does fall in the desert, cactuses can store the water for long periods of time.

The Sonoran Desert in southern Arizona

AMERICA'S GIANT CACTUS

The largest cactus in the United States is the saguaro (SWAR o). The saguaro is one of the largest cactuses in the world.

The saguaro can grow to 60 feet, taller than many trees. A big saguaro may weigh ten tons (20 thousand pounds). That is twice the weight of a bull elephant.

A saguaro stem may have several arms. They add to the saguaro's treelike look. In some parts of the desert, large numbers of saguaros make cactus forests.

The saguaro grows only in the deserts of Arizona, southeast California, and Sonora, Mexico.

A giant saguaro cactus

WILD ANIMALS AND CACTUSES

Many wild animals of the deserts use cactus plants. For woodpeckers and elf owls, the huge saguaro is a tree house. The birds nest in holes in the giant cactuses.

The cactus wren pulls spines and cactus joints to weave its nest. Somehow, the wren doesn't spear itself.

Bats, insects, and hummingbirds feed in the flowers of saguaros and other cactuses. The fruits and seeds of cactuses are important animal foods.

A cactus wren at its nest in a cholla cactus

CACTUS PARKS

In the deserts of the southwestern United States are huge, colorful wild gardens. Some of the finest areas have been set aside for cactus plants and other desert wildlife.

Organ Pipe Cactus National Monument in southern Arizona is one of the best cactus parks. This huge, wild park is named for its rare organ pipe cactuses.

Some other big parks for cactuses are California's Anza-Borrego State Park, Big Bend National Park in Texas, and Saguaro National Monument in Arizona.

Organ Pipe Cactus National Monument in southern Arizona

CACTUS PLANTS AND PEOPLE

Native American people of the deserts, such as the Papagos, use cactus fruit for syrup and wine. For most people though, cactuses are just curious plants—to be enjoyed from a safe distance.

Some people take cactus from the desert to sell. That practice has made some kinds of cactuses **endangered.** They are in danger of disappearing forever. Desert parks, however, help to protect many of our amazing cactuses.

Glossary

desert (DEHZ ert) — any land area of low, scattered rainfall during the year

endangered (en DANE jerd) — in danger of becoming extinct

joint (JOYNT) — a section of a cactus plant that can easily snap away from the rest of the plant

native (NAY tiv) — found naturally in an area

species (SPEE sheez) — within a group of closely related plants, one certain kind, such as *saguaro* cactus

INDEX